free and Independent *To all* to whom these presents shall come *Greeting*

Records remaining in our Secretarys Office do find there filed a certain Original Act

Act for supplying the City of New York with pure and wholesome Water." *Whereas* Daniel

for the purpose of supplying the City of New York with water for the use of such of the Inha

this laudable design and to divide the Hazards attendant thereon, set on foot a Sub

the Legislature should deem it expedient to grant them support and encouragement

suitable Charter of Incorporation, as doth appear by their several petitions to the Legislature

future Associates, may be encouraged to proceed to carry into effect their laudable undertaking

the Inhabitants of the said City. *Be it enacted by the People* of the State of New York

Joseph Browne and their present and future Associates, their successors and Assigns, be and

Directors of the Manhattan Company" and are hereby Ordained, Constituted and declared

they and their Successors shall and may have continual Succession, and shall be person

being answered unto, defending and being defended in all Courts and places whatsoever

they and their Successors may have a common Seal and make, Change and alter the same

shall be in Law capable of purchasing, holding and Conveying any Estate real and person

shall be such only as shall be necessary to promote or attain the objects of this incorporation.

exceed *Two Millions* of Dollars, and that a Share in the said Stock shall be fifty

under the direction of the said President and Directors until the whole Number of Shares

Shares, and shall further be kept open as aforesaid for the term of thirty days thereafter,

that it shall and may be Lawful for the Mayor Aldermen and Commonalty of the City

thousand. *And be it further enacted,* That the Stock, property and concerns of

and Citizens of the said City of New York of which Directors the Recorder of the said City

their Offices for one year from the second tuesday in December in every year; and twelve of the said

the day, and at such place within the City of New York, as a Majority of the directors for the time

thirty days previous to the time of holding the said Election by an advertisement to be inserted in at

tion shall be made by such of the Stockholders of the said Company as shall attend for that

lot; and the twelve persons who shall have the greatest number of Votes at any Election shall

an equal number of Votes in such manner that a greater number of persons than twelve shall

before authorized to Vote at such Elections shall proceed to Ballot a second time, and by

The history of JPMorgan Chase

Leadership in finance since 1799

Table of contents

Below: The Bank of The Manhattan Co. used various images of Oceanus, the Greek god of water, as its longtime symbol for more than 150 years. This sculpture of Oceanus, by artist Elie Nadelman (1882-1946), was installed above the main entrance to the bank's fourth and final building at 40 Wall Street in 1930.

Introduction

JPMorgan Chase & Co. is one of the world's oldest, largest and best-known financial institutions.

As a global financial services firm with operations in more than 60 countries, JPMorgan Chase & Co. combines two of the world's premier financial brands: J.P. Morgan and Chase. The firm is a leader across an array of financial services, including investment banking, commercial banking, credit cards, financial transaction processing and asset management. JPMorgan Chase & Co. serves millions of consumers in the United States and many of the world's most prominent corporate, institutional and government clients.

JPMorgan Chase & Co. is built on the foundation of more than 1,200 predecessor institutions that have come together through the years to form today's company. We trace our roots to 1799 in New York City, and our many well-known heritage firms include J.P. Morgan & Co., The Chase Manhattan Bank, Bank One, Manufacturers Hanover Trust Co., Chemical Bank, The First National Bank of Chicago, National Bank of Detroit, The Bear Stearns Companies Inc., Robert Fleming Holdings, Cazenove Group and the businesses acquired in the WaMu transaction. Each of these firms, in its time, was closely tied to innovations in finance and the growth of the U.S. and global economies.

The pages that follow provide highlights of the JPMorgan Chase & Co. story – our history, our predecessor institutions, our people, our services and our business principles.

The beginning: The Manhattan Co.

Commercial banking in the United States got its start immediately after the Revolutionary War. The earliest American banks played a central role in the nation's economic and industrial growth by lending money, safeguarding deposits and issuing bank notes that were used as currency.

The Bank of New York – founded in 1784 by Alexander Hamilton, who became President George Washington's treasury secretary – was the first commercial bank in New York City. It had no competition until 1799 when Hamilton's political rival, Aaron Burr, a U.S. senator and future vice president of the United States, founded The Bank of The Manhattan Co. JPMorgan Chase traces its beginnings to Burr's fledgling institution.

The Bank of The Manhattan Co. had an unusual beginning. Burr led a group of New Yorkers, including Hamilton, in obtaining a state charter for a company to supply fresh water to the residents of Lower Manhattan. At Burr's initiative, the charter

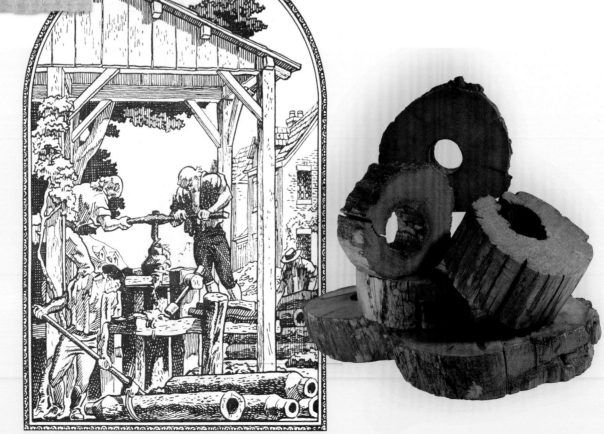

MANHATTAN COMPANY.
☞ The Office of Discount and Deposit will open for the transaction of business, for the present, at 10 o'clock in the forenoon, and continue open until 3 o'clock in the afternoon, when the business of the day will be closed.
HENRY REMSEN, Cashier.
September 24.

Above: Five months after The Manhattan Co. was chartered, the water company established a banking operation: an "Office of Discount and Deposit." This advertisement announcing the bank's business hours appeared in October 1799 in *The Mercantile Advisor,* a New York newspaper.

Right: Made from hollowed pine logs, The Manhattan Co.'s wooden water pipes carried fresh water to customers from a reservoir near the present City Hall. Six miles of pipes were laid in its first year of operation. For 43 years, the company supplied water to more than 2,000 customers in Lower Manhattan until New York City developed a municipal water system.

4

included a provision allowing the company to employ its excess capital in "any other monied transactions or operations, not inconsistent with the Constitution and laws of the United States." Burr then used that provision to start a bank.

The waterworks, called The Manhattan Co., laid a network of pipes made from hollowed pine logs and distributed water until 1842. The Bank of The Manhattan Co. outlived the waterworks and became one of the leading banking institutions in the nation – lending money and underwriting bonds, for instance, to help finance the Erie Canal, which opened in 1825.

The Hamilton-Burr duel

American statesmen Alexander Hamilton and Aaron Burr collaborated to establish The Manhattan Co. in 1799. However, Hamilton opposed Burr's provision in its charter enabling the water company to open a bank and severed his connection to the company. Their mutual antagonism over a variety of issues raged until 1804, when Burr challenged Hamilton to a duel. Hamilton was mortally wounded. The pistols were owned by Hamilton's brother-in-law, John Church, whose great-granddaughter sold them to The Bank of The Manhattan Co. in 1930. Today, they are part of the JPMorgan Chase Historical Collection.

5

Early growth of U.S. banks

As America expanded and diversified in the 1800s, new banks were formed across the nation. JPMorgan Chase has historic links to many of these early institutions, including The Western Reserve Bank of Warren, one of the first banks in Ohio when it was organized in 1812; Second State Bank of Indiana, formed in 1834 when Indianapolis still was a frontier town with a population of about 1,500; and Springfield Marine and Fire Insurance Co., which began operations in Illinois in 1851. Abraham Lincoln was one of Springfield Marine and Fire's first customers, depositing $310. All three institutions were predecessors of Bank One, which merged with JPMorgan Chase in 2004.

Individual states controlled the creation of banks in the early 1800s, and several states were highly restrictive in granting charters or gave them only to organizers who belonged to the political party in power. Demand for banking services was so great, however, that entrepreneurs sometimes found ways to get around such prohibitions.

In some instances, banks were offshoots of industrial or commercial businesses. New York Manufacturing Co. began in 1812 as a manufacturer of cotton processing equipment and switched to banking five years later. It was a forerunner of Manufacturers Hanover Trust Co. on the JPMorgan Chase family tree. In 1823, the New York Chemical Manufacturing Co. began producing medicines, paints and dyes at a plant in Greenwich Village. It modeled its charter on The Manhattan Co., using excess capital in 1824 to open a bank called The Chemical Bank, which joined the JPMorgan Chase family in 1996.

The Chemical Bank in New York sold its chemical manufacturing factory in 1851, continuing solely as a bank. The bank used this engraving of its factory – located on the Hudson River in what now is Midtown Manhattan – on stock certificates in the 1950s.

To sidestep Wisconsin's prohibition against banking, in 1839 Scottish immigrant George Smith founded the Wisconsin Marine and Fire Insurance Co., which, despite its name, operated like a bank by accepting deposits and issuing bank notes redeemable in gold.

The notes, known popularly as "George Smith's money," were used as currency throughout the Midwest. By one estimate, they represented nearly 75% of the currency in circulation in Chicago in 1854. Smith's company became the first legally approved bank in Wisconsin following statehood in 1848 and later was known as The Marine Corp., merging with JPMorgan Chase predecessor Bank One in 1988.

Right: The Wisconsin Marine and Fire Insurance Co. operated as an insurance business, received deposits, issued certificates and lent money. Its bank notes were widely circulated throughout the Midwest. The company became the first legal "bank" in Wisconsin in 1853 after the state's legislature passed an act authorizing banking.

SPRINGFIELD MARINE & FIRE INSURANCE C?

Right: Abraham Lincoln was Springfield Marine and Fire Insurance Co.'s most famous customer. He opened an account at the bank in 1853 while practicing law in Springfield, Illinois. Lincoln's account was particularly active in the years leading up to his election as U.S. president in 1860. He remained a customer throughout his presidency until his death in 1865. The account was closed two years later.

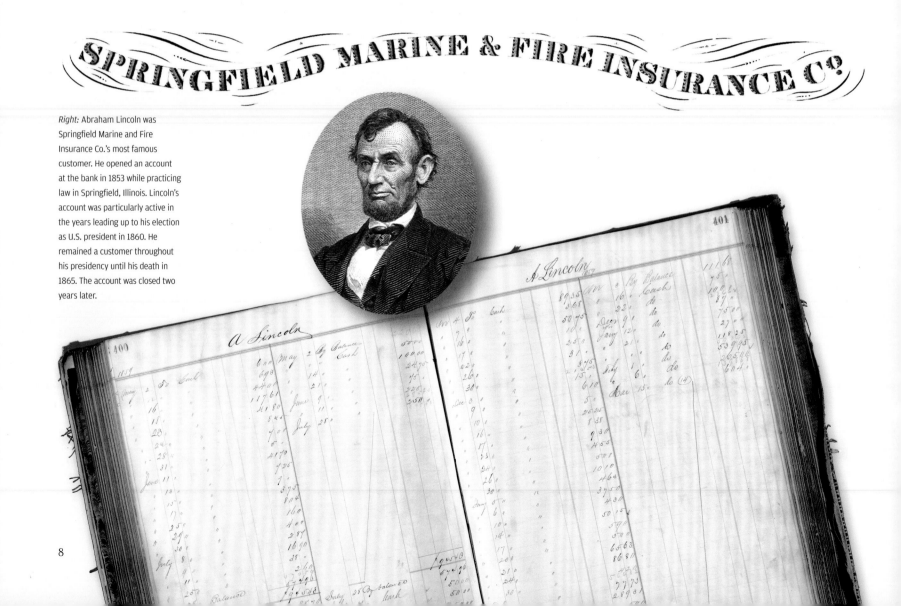

Below: In the aftermath of the Great Seattle Fire, money from San Francisco and from the East funneled into Seattle. Washington National Building Loan and Investment Association was founded in Seattle to help people rebuild houses, as commercial banks were reluctant to lend to homeowners.

Right: Twenty-five city blocks – more than 120 acres – in Seattle's business district were destroyed in the Great Seattle Fire of 1889. After the fire, wooden buildings were banned, replaced by brick structures.

Other banks were formed in response to specific local circumstances or needs. In Seattle, civic leaders created Washington National Building Loan and Investment Association in 1889 to supply mortgage loans to help rebuild the city following the Great Seattle Fire. The new company made history by issuing amortized monthly installment home loans, the first such loans on the Pacific Coast. Amortized mortgages were popular from the start. In a city with a population of 43,000 in 1890, nearly 2,000 Seattle residents used amortized loans from Washington National to build or buy homes during the next two decades. Washington National was renamed Washington Mutual Savings Bank in 1917 and was acquired by JPMorgan Chase in 2008.

9

National banking era

By 1860, just prior to the Civil War, the United States had more than 1,500 commercial banks with nearly $700 million of loans outstanding. The war brought challenge and change.

The United States did not have a unified national currency when the war began. Instead, individual banks – including our early predecessors – issued paper money in the form of notes. Although this system had served the nation well in its formative years, more than 7,000 different types of bank notes – of various shapes, sizes and colors – were in circulation, resulting in confusion and inefficiency. The situation changed in 1862 when the Union began printing "greenback" currency to help finance the war.

However, many Americans considered greenbacks worthless because they were supported by the credit of the government, not by gold or silver. Their instability required a strong system of federal regulation and control so, in 1863, the United States passed the National Banking Act, adopting a dual system of federal and state chartered banks. Under the act, only national banks that bought U.S. government bonds and deposited them with the U.S. Treasury could print notes.

One of the pioneering institutions was The First National Bank of Chicago, which received federal charter Number 8 in 1863. First National became part

Below: Before the U.S. government adopted a national currency and began printing paper notes, those issued by individual state banks had little or no government regulation. While legal tender, bank notes came in a variety of designs, as seen in these samples issued by JPMorgan Chase predecessors.

of Bank One in 1998. Other predecessors founded or reorganized in the wake of the National Banking Act include Hanover National Bank (New York), The Indiana National Bank (Indianapolis), The National Bank of Commerce (New York) and Union National Bank (Chicago).

Initially, only a handful of banks applied for a national charter, but the trickle became a flood in 1865 when the federal government began imposing a 10% tax on bank notes issued by state banks. By 1868, there were only 247 state banks left in the United States, compared with 1,640 national banks.

Many thought that state banks would disappear altogether, but a surprising turnaround occurred: Forced to find a substitute for notes, state banks invented interest-paying demand deposits (deposits that could be withdrawn at any time). With this new service at their disposal, state banks rebounded and outnumbered national banks by 1894.

Below: In 1878, Chase National Bank moved to 104 Broadway in New York after operating in a one-room office during the preceding year. Chase was the first bank in the city to choose a location other than Wall Street.

Left: John Thompson (1802-1891), a strong advocate of the national banking system, founded Chase National Bank with his son, Samuel. John Thompson was well-known in the banking community as a publisher of counterfeit detectors (journals used to identify fraudulent signatures on bank notes) and of *The Bank Note Reporter*, today's *American Banker*.

Above: By the 1890s, Chase National had grown into a "banker's bank," providing correspondent services to other banks across the nation and establishing relationships with individuals and corporations throughout the United States. In 1896, Chase National moved to larger offices in the Italian Renaissance-style New York Clearing House building two blocks from Wall Street, where it remained until 1914.

The founding of Chase National Bank

During the severe economic downturn in the decade following the American Civil War, John Thompson, a 75-year-old Wall Street publisher and banker, established Chase National Bank in a one-room office in Manhattan in 1877. Thompson named the bank in honor of his late friend, Salmon P. Chase, who had not only been President Lincoln's treasury secretary but also had served as governor of Ohio and chief justice of the United States.

Chase National Bank soon became a respected correspondent bank (a bank that performed services for other banks) and expanded rapidly in the early 20th century by developing a large corporate business. By 1930, it was the world's largest bank, with assets of $2.7 billion. In 1955, Chase National merged with The Bank of The Manhattan Co. to form The Chase Manhattan Bank.

Right: The 1864 painting *First Reading of the Emancipation Proclamation of President Lincoln* by artist Francis Bicknell Carpenter (1830-1900) depicts Lincoln with his Cabinet; Secretary of the Treasury Salmon P. Chase stands behind him to his right. The painting is in the collection of the U.S. Senate.

Far right: Salmon P. Chase (1808-1873), secretary of the treasury under President Lincoln, is the namesake of Chase National Bank. He was instrumental in establishing the national banking system in 1863, a year after securing passage of the Legal Tender Act. The marble bust of Chase by artist Thomas Dow Jones (1811-1881), from 1875, is part of the JPMorgan Chase Historical Collection. A duplicate is installed in the U.S. Supreme Court Building in Washington, D.C.

Below: As an American banker in London, Junius S. Morgan (1813-1890), father of J. Pierpont Morgan, set the future direction of the Morgan firms: multinational, wholesale and quality private banking. Junius' astute financial advice earned the respect of his peers on both sides of the Atlantic in the 1850s and 1860s. European investors trusted him as a dealer of U.S. securities, and American railroad companies sought him out as a highly valued advisor.

Junius made his reputation as a sovereign lender with J.S. Morgan & Co.'s successful 1870 loan to the French provisional government during the Franco-Prussian War. After helping his son, Pierpont, establish a private banking firm in New York City, Junius Morgan remained a critical connection for the Morgan firms' international business.

Origins of J.P. Morgan & Co.

JPMorgan Chase's other namesake predecessor, J.P. Morgan & Co., was founded in New York in 1871 by 34-year-old J. Pierpont Morgan and banker Anthony J. Drexel. The firm originally was called Drexel, Morgan & Co. but changed its name to J.P. Morgan & Co. in 1895 after Anthony Drexel's death.

J. Pierpont Morgan is one of the most famous and influential investment bankers in American history. Morgan grew up in the banking business: His father, Junius, headed J.S. Morgan & Co., the most prominent American-owned private bank in London and the leading issuer of American securities in England. Junius was involved in many landmark transactions, such as raising money for the first trans-Atlantic cable project in 1858. But his real breakthrough came in 1870, when his firm arranged a $50 million loan for the French provisional government during the Franco-Prussian War. Other banks questioned whether the loan ever would be repaid, but Junius knew that no French government since 1789 had defaulted on its debts. Junius was correct in his judgment: France repaid the entire $50 million ahead of schedule. His astute decision propelled J.S. Morgan & Co. into the upper ranks of international finance.

Before co-founding Drexel, Morgan & Co., J. Pierpont Morgan worked as J.S. Morgan & Co.'s New York agent and learned under the tutelage of his father. He soon became one of America's most powerful and influential bankers, heading what became America's pre-eminent private bank.

Left: Drexel, Morgan & Co. was located at 23 Wall Street at the corner of Wall Street and Broad Street — the crossroads of New York's financial district in Lower Manhattan.

Far right: This 1874 Drexel, Morgan & Co. ad from *Bankers Almanac* highlighted the firm's offices in New York, London, Paris and Philadelphia.

Anthony J. Drexel (1826-1893) already was a prominent Philadelphia-based private banker when Junius Morgan approached him to form a business partnership with his son, Pierpont. The alliance with Drexel, which had an office in Paris, gave the Morgan firm a foothold in financial markets in four cities in Europe and America.

By the time J. Pierpont Morgan (1837-1913) became senior partner of Drexel, Morgan at the age of 34, he was a recognized Wall Street figure in his own right, a man of many diversified business interests with a substantial record of accomplishments.

BANKING HOUSE OF
DREXEL, MORGAN & CO.,
Corner of Wall and Broad Streets,
NEW YORK.
Erected 1872-3.

DREXEL & CO.,
PHILADELPHIA.
DREXEL, HARJES & CO.,
PARIS.
AGENTS AND ATTORNEYS OF
MESSRS. J. S. MORGAN & CO., LONDON.
DRAW EXCHANGE AT CUSTOMARY USANCES.
Issue Commercial and Travelers' Credits.

Investments in railroads and industry

Drexel, Morgan & Co. specialized initially as an agent for Europeans investing in the United States, working closely with J.S. Morgan & Co. in London to raise much of the capital to support America's industrial expansion. The two firms, together with affiliates in Paris and Philadelphia, quickly gained the confidence of Europeans for the ability to identify sound, profitable American investments.

The Morgan firms were known in particular for their investments in railroads, the largest and most dynamic American industry in the years after the Civil War. In a historic transaction, Drexel, Morgan sold stock in American financier William Vanderbilt's New York Central Railroad in 1879 without driving down the share price. The deal involved the largest block of stock ever offered at that time – 250,000 shares – and highlighted J. Pierpont Morgan's strength as a mobilizer of capital and wholesaler of securities.

By the late 19th century, railroads in the United States were plagued by overcapacity and rate wars. Morgan saw opportunity in the situation. He became an industry consolidator, reorganizing financially troubled railroads by cutting their costs, restructuring their debt, placing their stock in trusts he managed and appointing senior executives who were loyal to him. This process, which came to be called "Morganization," was applied to the Northern Pacific, the Erie, the Reading and many other railroads. By the end of his career, J. Pierpont Morgan had "Morganized" approximately one-sixth of the track in the United States.

Below left: Northern Pacific Railway Company was one of the many financially troubled railroads J. Pierpont Morgan restructured in the late 19th century. Morgan was regarded as a leader in reorganizing struggling railroad companies. As a result, American railroad bonds were among the nation's safest investments in the 19th century.

Far left: The $5 million check signed by American financier William Vanderbilt is connected to the purchase of New York Central Railroad stock in 1879.

Left: J. Pierpont Morgan became one of America's most powerful and influential bankers. His ability to judge the new-issues market and to determine which offerings would sell, and at what price, was among his strongest skills as a banker.

Steel soon succeeded railroads as the largest and most important American industry, and J. Pierpont Morgan left his imprint there as well. In 1901, he established the U.S. Steel Corporation by merging U.S. steel giant Carnegie Steel Works and some 33 other companies, including steamship lines, ore mines, wire mills, plate and tubing companies, and several railroads. The deal was unprecedented, valuing U.S. Steel at a market capitalization of $1.4 billion – the first billion-dollar corporation in world history.

Morgan also engineered significant mergers in other industries, creating General Electric (1892), maker of electrical products, and International Harvester (1902), maker of farm equipment. In addition, he helped finance public service companies and emerging industrial giants such as AT&T (1906). One observer described Morgan as "the mightiest force in American business life."

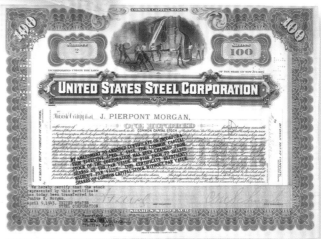

In 1878, Drexel, Morgan in New York became the banker for the Edison Electric Light Company. Excited by Thomas Edison's invention, J. Pierpont Morgan installed electricity in Drexel, Morgan's offices and in his Madison Avenue townhouse, the first private residence in New York City entirely illuminated by Edison's incandescent lights. In this image of Morgan's private study, the highlighted circles identify electric fixtures.

Thomas Alva Edison
(1847-1931)

Financing governments abroad

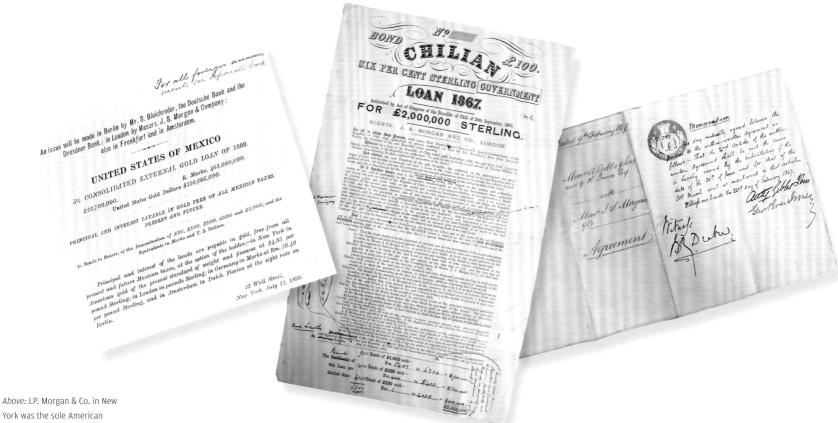

Above: J.P. Morgan & Co. in New York was the sole American issuer of the Mexican 5% external consolidated gold loan of 1899. The success of the issue added to the firm's prestige, attracting business from other foreign governments, as well as from large overseas corporations.

Middle and right: J.S. Morgan & Co. in London sponsored its first major international loan to the Chilean government in 1867. Proving it was able to serve the needs of a government, Morgan was appointed the loan's London agent, responsible for holding the Chilean government's deposits and paying the loan interest to English bondholders. The work provided the firm with a steady source of income and led to other Chilean government loans.

By the final decade of the 19th century, J.P. Morgan & Co. (as the firm was renamed in 1895) had become a leader in international finance, raising billions of dollars for foreign companies and governments and establishing a global investment banking heritage that continues at JPMorgan Chase today. Morgan's New York and London offices oversaw accounts for governments on almost every continent.

The Morgan firms sponsored their first major international loan to the government of Chile in 1867. That transaction and the successful 1870 loan to the government of France were managed by J.S. Morgan & Co. in London, which also oversaw the firms' participation in European government loans to Norway (1886), Turkey (1890), Russia (1891), Spain (1892) and Germany (1899).

Morgan also participated in loans to Central and South American governments. Beginning in the 1880s, both the New York and London offices developed long-standing relationships with the government of Argentina. Morgan became one of the Argentine government's principal foreign bankers, leading every major financing for the nation throughout the 1890s.

In 1899, J.P. Morgan & Co. in New York co-managed an issue of bonds for the Mexican government, marking the first time the name of an American banking house appeared on a foreign loan prospectus. Between 1900 and 1910, the Morgan firms sponsored dozens of foreign government loans, including offerings for China, Italy, Finland, Portugal, Sweden, Greece, India, Thailand and New Zealand. J. Pierpont Morgan himself decided which accounts the Morgan firms accepted, as well as the terms of their participation.

Financing major projects

Many of JPMorgan Chase's predecessor firms played important roles in the U.S. economy during the late 19th and early 20th centuries, an era of memorable engineering projects and revolutionary technologies.

The Brooklyn Trust Co. was a major lender for the construction of the Brooklyn Bridge, completed in 1883 and, at the time, the world's longest suspension bridge. William L. Strong, founder of The New York Security & Trust Co., was a member of the American finance committee that raised funds for the Statue of Liberty's pedestal, the largest 19th century concrete structure in the United States. In 1904, J.P. Morgan & Co. helped finance the Panama Canal, arranging for the transfer of $40 million for the U.S. government to buy land rights from the bankrupt French Panama Canal Co. The purchase was the largest real estate transaction in history.

In 1911, Union National Bank, South Texas National Bank and Commercial National Bank, predecessors of legacy institution Texas Commerce Bancshares, Inc., helped finance the construction of the 50-mile-long Houston Ship Channel, one of the largest public projects in the Southwest. Houston developer Jesse Jones, a director and major stockholder of Union National, persuaded other Houston banks to purchase unsold municipal bonds issued to finance the channel's construction. The Houston Ship Channel opened in 1914 to great fanfare and, today, is one of the busiest waterways in the United States.

Below: The Brooklyn Trust Co., a JPMorgan Chase predecessor, helped finance construction of New York's Brooklyn Bridge, which opened in 1883. Spanning the East River, the historic bridge was the first to connect Manhattan and Brooklyn.

Right: The 47-mile-long Panama Canal, which connects the Atlantic Ocean and the Pacific Ocean, was one of the largest engineering projects ever undertaken. Built between 1904 and 1914, the canal saved ships from traveling the 8,000-mile journey around the southern tip of South America.

Far right: The pedestal for the Statue of Liberty was partly financed by a group that included the president of The New York Security & Trust Co. This bank later merged with The Liberty National Bank, which used the statue as its logo between 1891 and 1921. Both banks are predecessors of JPMorgan Chase.

Banking at the beginning of the 20th century

J.P. Morgan & Co.'s headquarters at 23 Wall Street was situated in the heart of New York City's financial district. In 1912, J. Pierpont Morgan planned a new structure on the site. Completed in 1914 after his death, the Neoclassical structure embodied the firm's characteristically discreet business style. The Morgan name was deliberately left off the building's façade, and the entrance doors bore only the number "23." It was known simply as "the Corner" – a measure of Morgan's prominence in the world of finance.

Banking at the dawn of the 20th century was different in many ways from today. Most states – the primary banking regulators at the turn of the century – prohibited or severely restricted branching, fearing that small banks might have trouble competing with large banks if branching was allowed. As a result, the United States was a nation of one-office banks, the vast majority of which were small institutions.

In 1898, New York became one of the first states to permit branch banking on a limited scale when it allowed New York City banks to have branches anywhere in the city's five boroughs. The Corn Exchange Bank, a predecessor of Chemical Bank, quickly capitalized on the new rules, opening a dozen branches within four years and changing its focus from providing credit to grain merchants to serving retail customers. When New York City opened its subway system in 1904, the bank opened branch offices in residential areas along the subway lines to serve commuters.

For J.P. Morgan & Co., the first decade of the 20th century was among the busiest in the bank's history as the number and size of the security offerings Morgan placed exceeded those of any bank in Europe or America.

Pictured are images of JPMorgan Chase predecessors from around the nation at the turn of the 20th century. *Top*: First National Bank of Mantua, Ohio and Fourth National Bank, New York (with porters carrying a currency chest in 1910). *Center*: National Exchange Bank, Milwaukee, Wisconsin. *Bottom*: South Texas National Bank.

Elegant Beaux Arts building interiors were fashionable in banks built at the turn of the 20th century, as illustrated in the monumental interior of National Park Bank in New York, ca. 1929. The bronze teller cage and desk calendar, ca. 1931-1932, are from The First National Bank of Chicago's branch, and the table leg, ca. 1920, is from Lincoln Alliance Bank's branch in Rochester, New York.

Morgan's role as central banker

With his integrity, judgment and influence, J. Pierpont Morgan became America's unofficial central banker, personally intervening in business disputes and orchestrating solutions to economic crises.

During the Panic of 1893, President Grover Cleveland enlisted Morgan to stem the depletion of the nation's gold reserves. Europeans began withdrawing gold from the United States as economic conditions worsened. By late 1894, the U.S. gold reserve had fallen below $100 million, causing widespread concern that the value of the dollar, which was backed by gold, would be undermined. Morgan formed a syndicate to buy gold in Europe and bring it back to the United States. As each shipment arrived, the syndicate purchased 30-year bonds from the U.S. government and paid with gold, replenishing the government's stockpile of the precious metal and setting the stage for an economic recovery.

Morgan intervened again during the Panic of 1907, which began when several New York financial institutions teetered on the brink of insolvency, threatening the stability of the nation's economy. Morgan convinced New York's healthiest banks to provide money to the weakest banks to stop further failures. His efforts saved several trust companies and a leading brokerage house, bailed out the city of New York and rescued the New York Stock Exchange. The panic soon ran its course.

In response, Congress created the National Monetary Commission to recommend changes to the nation's monetary and banking structure. In 1913, based in large part on the commission's report, Congress established the Federal Reserve System to regulate the money supply and manage the economy. The Federal Reserve formally assumed the role of central banker that had been held informally by Morgan for years. The Federal Reserve Act also gave national banks the right to make real estate loans and exercise trust powers.

Morgan died just months before the Federal Reserve came into being. In an obituary, *The New York Times* reported, "With his unmatched abilities, with his character and the confidence he inspired, and with his power to organize and command, it was inevitable that he should be the leader, the builder-up in the domain of American finance. The growth in his time was prodigious, and now Wall Street is beyond the need or the possibility of one-man leadership."

J. Pierpont Morgan was succeeded as the head of J.P. Morgan & Co. by his son, J.P. "Jack" Morgan, Jr., a senior partner at the firm and an influential banker in his own right.

The World War I years

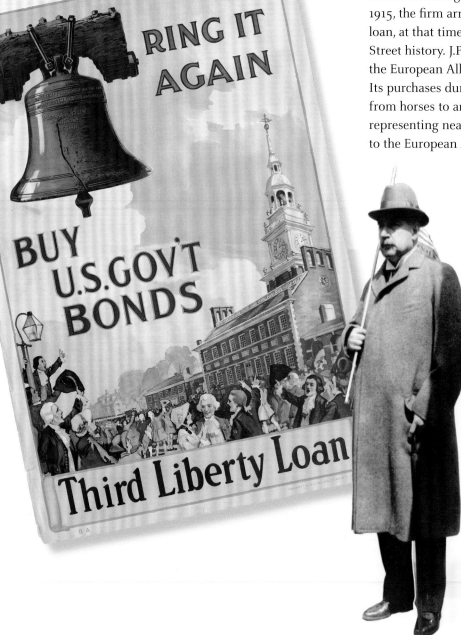

In the devastating years of World War I, a number of bank employees joined the armed forces – and many gave their lives. J.P. Morgan & Co. played a significant role in financing the Allied victory. In September 1915, the firm arranged a $500 million Anglo-French loan, at that time the largest foreign loan in Wall Street history. J.P. Morgan & Co. also was chosen by the European Allies as their U.S. purchasing agent. Its purchases during the war – involving everything from horses to artillery shells – totaled $3 billion, representing nearly half of all American supplies sold to the European Allies.

Left: Patriotic imagery was used extensively in bond posters to spur sales, as in this one from 1918. Many JPMorgan Chase & Co. predecessors were active in the distribution of U.S. government war bonds that helped finance the American war effort.

Below middle: Jack Morgan attended bond rallies and parades in New York City along with other prominent New York bankers to promote the purchase of bonds.

Opposite right, top: In 1918, Guaranty Trust Company of New York created an armored mobile bank for use behind the battle lines in France. As Guaranty's Paris office acted as a paying agent for the Army and Navy, the mobile bank enabled U.S. soldiers and sailors at the front to cash their checks or buy drafts on the spot.

Opposite right, bottom: Guaranty employees posed at an officers' training camp in Plattsburgh, New York, in 1917.

JPMorgan Chase predecessor Guaranty Trust Company of New York also buttressed the Allied cause. Its Paris office, which remained open throughout the war, was the first branch of an American bank in a foreign country to be designated a depository for the U.S. government. Guaranty also became a leading issuer of acceptances, which facilitated the flow of supplies abroad. In 1916, the total of Guaranty acceptances outstanding was twice that of any other bank in the United States.

The war, at the same time, was a watershed for the U.S. economy and the nation's banks. The United States was a net debtor nation when the war began in Europe in 1914. After the war, with many parts of Europe in ruins and desperately in need of reconstruction loans, the United States supplied much of the capital and became a net creditor nation. In the process, New York emerged as the world's leading capital market.

Right: Before the United States entered World War I, J.P. Morgan & Co. aided the British and French governments, arranging a $500 million loan that was offered to investors in the United States. Britain's King George V sent this cable personally thanking Jack Morgan for his wartime help.

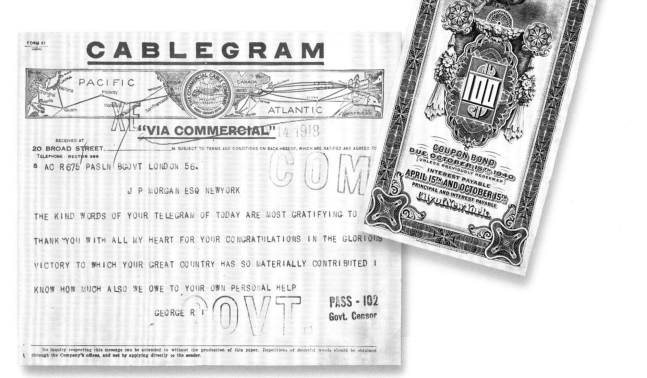

27

The roaring '20s

The U.S. banking industry changed dramatically in the 1920s, a decade of innovation and diversification. Many banks formed investment departments to meet customer demand for government and corporate securities. Some large banks went beyond the marketing of securities and established underwriting affiliates. The Chase National Bank and Guaranty Trust Company of New York became major players in the underwriting business – Chase in 1917 through its Chase Securities Corp. affiliate and Guaranty Trust through its Guaranty Co. affiliate, established four years later.

Guaranty Trust also opened the way for Americans to own foreign stocks by inventing the American depositary receipt (ADR) in 1927. Until then, investing in foreign equities was difficult because of currency exchange costs and other complexities, including a requirement that shares be presented at company offices overseas to collect dividends. Guaranty Trust resolved this issue by holding shares of foreign companies in its overseas offices. It then issued receipts, or ADRs, representing ownership of the shares. ADRs still trade in the United States in dollars and pay dividends in dollars.

Guaranty created the first ADR for British retailer Selfridges. Today, more than eight decades later, ADRs remain a principal way for Americans to invest

Below: In the 1920s, many commercial banks entered the securities business by creating subsidiaries in response to increased demand from corporations to raise capital through securities issues.

Below left: This illustration was printed on the cover of a 1929 Equitable Trust Company client brochure, which promoted services offered by the bank's Trust Department.

Right: Wall Street was transformed by skyscrapers in the 1920s, many of which were built by our predecessors. This etching by artist Anton Schutz (1894-1977) captures two: in the center, The Bank of The Manhattan Co.'s 71-story skyscraper, completed in 1930; to its left, Chase National's 1928 skyscraper, smaller, but with dramatic setbacks on its upper floors. J.P. Morgan & Co.'s 1914 headquarters at the corner of Wall Street and Broad Street is visible in the lower right.

in non-U.S. stocks. JPMorgan Chase & Co. continues to be the leading ADR depositary bank.

Diversification took banks into other areas beyond securities underwriting. In 1919, The First National Bank of Chicago created an affiliate, First National Investment Co., which invested in second mortgages and operated a travel agency.

The 1920s also saw a wave of bank mergers, failures and voluntary liquidations, with the result that the number of banks in the United States declined by 20% from 1921 to 1929.

Above: In the 1920s, Guaranty Trust Company was a leading corporate transfer agent. In 1926, the bank's Stock Bookkeeping Department introduced "time-saving" machines to prepare dividend checks for corporate stockholders.

Expanding to Europe, Latin America and Asia

The years during the 1920s were a time of global expansion. Guaranty Trust Company of New York had been an early pioneer, opening an agency office in London in 1892 to support its growing business in the financing of commodities and foreign trade. In 1897, Guaranty converted the office to a full-fledged branch and subsequently opened branches in Liverpool, Paris, Le Havre, Brussels, Antwerp and Manila.

But the big rush of American banks abroad took place after passage of the Federal Reserve Act of 1913, which removed many legal obstacles to the chartering of overseas branches. Ironically, some banks suddenly found it easier to establish branch offices in distant lands than to overcome state anti-branching laws and open branches at home.

Latin American and Asian markets were considered especially promising in the 1920s at a time when Europe still was recovering from World War I. In 1917, Chase National Bank invested in American Foreign Banking Corporation, which had developed a network of 19 foreign branches. When American

Left: Guaranty Trust Company of New York, which later merged with J.P. Morgan & Co., had several branches in London by the 1920s. In its advertising, Guaranty heavily promoted the bank's range of services abroad to its American clients, both commercial customers and leisure travelers.

Below: The Equitable Trust Company was the first American bank to open a branch on the European continent when it established a Paris branch in 1910.

Paris

Shanghai

San Juan

London

Chase National Bank's foreign branches, such as those in Paris, Shanghai, San Juan and London, offered full-service banking, including trade financing and government loans. This London photograph shows foreign exchange dealers at work at Chase National's 10 Moorgate office in 1932.

Foreign went out of business in 1925, Chase National bought three of the branches – in Havana, Panama City and Cristobal (Panama Canal Zone).

Meanwhile, The Equitable Trust Company of New York opened branches in Mexico City, London, Paris, Hong Kong, Shanghai and Tianjin, all of which became part of Chase National when the two companies merged. As a result, Chase began the 1930s with one of the banking industry's largest overseas branch systems, with a presence in Europe, Latin America and Asia.

The Chase-Equitable merger not only created the world's largest bank in terms of assets and deposits but also gave the Rockefeller family, which controlled Equitable, a strong connection to Chase. The Rockefellers have been associated with the firm ever since.

The 1929 market crash and the Great Depression

Although the banking industry had an abundance of money to lend in the 1920s, large corporations borrowed less, choosing instead to finance a sizable portion of their capital needs in the stock and bond markets. Consequently, banks in the United States sought new lending outlets, including loans to individuals speculating in the stock market.

As the stock market rose, these loans produced solid returns. But when the market crashed in October 1929, many of the loans went into default. For the banking industry, the 1930s would be the most difficult period in history to date.

In the years after the crash, thousands of banks faced hard times because of loan losses, depositor withdrawals, inadequate reserves and, in some cases, the collapse of speculative investments made in the 1920s. Even well-capitalized, well-managed institutions were battered by the financial panics that swept across the nation.

Washington Mutual Savings Bank in Seattle experienced a bank run in 1931 when depositors confused it with a similarly named bank that went out of business. The bank arranged an emergency infusion of cash to pay all the withdrawals in full and stayed open late to meet every withdrawal request. These and other actions helped soothe customers' frayed nerves, and the run ended two days after it had started.

Several other JPMorgan Chase predecessors endured similar crises. In June 1932, depositors began withdrawing money from The First National Bank of Chicago – the city's largest bank – when unknown individuals circulated flyers claiming First National was insolvent. Media reports speculated that the attacks were the work of political enemies of First National's

president, Melvin Traylor, considered a potential Democratic Party nominee for U.S. president. Traylor responded to the attacks with an impassioned speech attesting to First National's soundness, ending the run.

Other predecessors helped rescue failing banks. In Houston, two of the city's major banks were on the brink of collapse in October 1931. National Bank of Commerce President Jesse Jones called a meeting of the city's bank leaders, urging them to pool $1.25 million to save the failing institutions. Some of the bankers did not want to risk any of their limited capital, but Jones argued that allowing the two banks to collapse might bring down the entire banking sector in the city. A rescue finally was agreed, including the absorption of one of the failing banks by Jones' National Bank of Commerce. Because of his leadership, not a single bank in Houston collapsed during the Great Depression.

Below left: A *New York Times* article from October 24, 1929, one day after the devastating stock market crash in New York, reported on the efforts of J.P. Morgan & Co. and Chase National Bank to buy blue chip stocks to halt the stock sell-off and stabilize the market. Unfortunately, actions taken by these firms could not quell the escalating fears of panicked investors.

Background photo: Images of breadlines – unemployed men and women queuing for free food on street corners – exemplified the desperation many Americans experienced during the Great Depression.

WORST STOCK CRASH STEMMED BY BANKS;
12,894,650-SHARE DAY SWAMPS MARKET;
LEADERS CONFER, FIND CONDITIONS SOUND

FINANCIERS EASE TENSION | Wall Street Optimistic After Stormy Day; Clerical Work May Force Holiday Tomorrow | LOSSES RECOVERED IN PART

Below left: On March 24, 1933, customers mobbed the new National Bank of Detroit to open 562 accounts on the bank's opening day following six weeks without banking services in Detroit. Customers brought in bundles of currency and coins that ranged from a few hundred dollars to several hundred thousand dollars.

Below right: Many First National Bank of Chicago customers wrote letters to Melvin Traylor, the bank's president, thanking him for inspiring confidence and offering him their support.

While thousands of banks across the country went out of business during the 1930s, JPMorgan Chase predecessor National Bank of Detroit was formed at the very depths of the Great Depression. After Michigan's governor declared an eight-day bank holiday in February 1933 – closing all of Michigan's banks so they could regroup financially – Detroit's two largest banks lacked the funds to reopen, leaving the city virtually without banking services for the next six weeks. General Motors Corporation and the Reconstruction Finance Corporation, the federal government agency that provided emergency financing to banks, stepped into this void to establish National Bank of Detroit.

Local corporations and consumers, desperate for checking services, flocked to the new institution. On the bank's first day, Chrysler Corporation deposited $4 million, General Motors $1 million and General Electric $500,000. The two founding institutions divested their ownership in the 1940s, and National Bank of Detroit grew into the largest bank in Michigan. It merged with First Chicago Corp. in 1995 to form First Chicago NBD Corp.

Investment banks and brokerage firms also faced perilous times. Many went out of business after the stock market collapsed, but JPMorgan Chase predecessor Bear Stearns – which had been founded in 1923 to trade equities and government securities – was one of the few that continued to expand. Trading fell sharply, but the firm had accumulated enough capital to maintain its New York office, avoid any employee layoffs and even pay bonuses. By 1933, the firm had grown from its original seven employees to 75. That same year, it opened its first branch office in Chicago.

33

"First-class business ... in a first-class way"

In May 1933, J.P. "Jack" Morgan, Jr., as well as several Morgan partners and other major bank executives, testified at hearings held by the U.S. Senate Banking Committee investigating the causes of the 1929 stock market crash and the subsequent banking crisis. The hearings questioned the role banks played in the speculative fever leading up to the crash.

J.P. Morgan & Co. was the first bank investigated, and Jack Morgan was the first witness to represent the firm. In his opening statement, Jack Morgan empha-

sized with great dignity the duties and ethics of the private banker upheld by three generations of Morgans at the firm and still a cornerstone of JPMorgan Chase & Co. today.

"If I may be permitted to speak of the firm of which I have the honor to be the senior partner," Morgan said, "I should state that at all times the idea of doing only first-class business, and that in a first-class way, has been before our minds. We have never been satisfied with simply keeping within the law, but have constantly sought so to act that we might fully observe the professional code, and so maintain the credit and reputation which has been handed down to us from our predecessors in the firm."

In May 1933, J.P. "Jack" Morgan, Jr., who had become the senior partner of J.P. Morgan & Co. following his father's death in 1913, testified at a series of Senate committee hearings. He publicly stated the guiding principle of the firm — to conduct "first-class business ... in a first-class way."

Glass-Steagall

In the wake of the banking crisis, U.S. President Franklin D. Roosevelt's administration sought legislation to reduce banking risk. Congress responded by passing the Banking Act of 1933. Popularly known as Glass-Steagall, the act created federal deposit insurance, prohibited the payment of interest on checking accounts, and authorized the Federal Reserve to impose a ceiling on the interest banks could pay on time deposits and savings accounts. Equally important, the law erected a wall in the United States between commercial banking (taking deposits and making loans) and investment banking (underwriting securities).

Three of JPMorgan Chase's predecessors, in particular, had to make a choice. J.P. Morgan & Co., which engaged in commercial banking activities in addition to underwriting securities, decided to continue as a commercial bank. Morgan spun off its securities underwriting business in newly formed Morgan Stanley & Co., headed by Morgan partners Henry Morgan – Jack Morgan's younger son – and Harold Stanley.

Guaranty Trust Company of New York, which also had a major presence in commercial and investment banking, closed its securities affiliate and underwriting business. Morgan and Guaranty merged in 1959 to create Morgan Guaranty Trust Co. of New York, later forming a holding company that revived the famous J.P. Morgan & Co. name.

For Chase National Bank, the decision was relatively easy. Its newly elected chairman, Winthrop Aldrich, had spoken out publicly in favor of driving a wedge between commercial and investment banking. Chase National complied immediately with this law, closing or spinning off all its Chase securities affiliates.

Senator Carter Glass (D-VA) (*left*) and Representative Henry B. Steagall (D-AL) (*below*) were the co-sponsors of the Banking Act of 1933.

35

World War II

The banking industry recovered from the trauma of the early 1930s and began to stabilize. In 1933, the worst year of the crisis, more than 4,000 U.S. banks failed, but in 1934, there were just 61 failures, and over the next eight years, only 53 institutions, on average, failed annually.

With the onset of war in Europe in 1939, many JPMorgan Chase predecessors helped the Allied cause, as they had during World War I.

In 1939, J.P. Morgan & Co. was chosen by the British and French governments to sell $1.5 billion of publicly traded securities in the New York market. The deal was sensitive for two reasons: Neither nation wanted its enemies to know that cash was being raised, and both wanted to sell the securities without affecting market prices. Only a few people at J.P. Morgan were aware of the sellers' identities, and the transactions remained a closely guarded secret for years.

After the United States entered the war in 1941, U.S. commercial banks became the leading distributors of war bonds, which were sold in denominations as small as $10. By war's end, more than 60% of the American population had bought at least one war bond, with total purchases coming to $186 billion.

Tens of thousands of bank employees served in the military during the war. As men left their jobs to enlist, banks appointed women to positions previously held by men – an early, small erosion of the traditional male dominance of banking in the United States.

The Great Depression had highlighted the need for increased global cooperation to avoid another worldwide economic collapse. Toward the end of World War II, policymakers in the United States, Great Britain and other nations began to develop an international system aimed at promoting financial stability and encouraging global trade.

These developments, combined with advances in communications and travel and the emergence of the Eurodollar (deposits denominated in U.S. dollars that are held by banks outside the United States, mainly in Europe), opened the way for global banking.

Above: During World War II, Valley National Bank, the largest bank in Arizona, offered loans of up to $300 to airmen stationed at Arizona airfields, enabling them to travel on home leaves. One hundred percent of the airmen repaid their loans.

Bottom left: On the eve of World War II, J.P. "Jack" Morgan, Jr., corresponded with British Prime Minister Neville Chamberlain, assuring him that J.P. Morgan & Co. was ready to serve the British government in any way it could. Shown is Chamberlain's response.

Bottom right: Chase National Bank's October 1945 employee newsletter welcomed home employees who served during wartime. At the end of World War II, JPMorgan Chase predecessors rehired employees, offered special loans to veterans and provided banking services to servicemen stationed abroad. On the home front, Red Cross arm bands were given to air raid wardens at Manufacturers Trust Co. in New York.

10, Downing Street,
Whitehall.

29th August, 1939.

Dear Mr. Morgan,

I am greatly obliged to you for your letter of August 28th and for the assurance you have sent to me and the Government of the readiness of your Company to do all that you can to help us if unhappily war comes.

I am most grateful to you for this assurance and for the personal message which you sent me.

Yours sincerely,

Neville Chamberlain.

The rise of global banking

Postwar globalization began slowly, building on the initial round of globalization that had taken place in the 1920s. By 1965, 12 U.S. banks maintained branches outside the United States. These included five predecessors of JPMorgan Chase: The Chase Manhattan Bank, Chemical Bank, The First National Bank of Chicago, Manufacturers Hanover Trust Co. and Morgan Guaranty Trust Co. of New York.

As thousands of American industrial companies expanded overseas, American banks followed to meet the companies' needs. Banks also recognized an opportunity to borrow Eurodollars, a major new pool of funds. By 1980, some 160 U.S. banks were operating branches or representative offices outside the United States. In turn, many banks in Europe, Asia and other regions extended their operations to the United States, completing the circle of the globalization of banking.

The Chase Manhattan Bank was a pioneer. In 1947, at the invitation of U.S. military authorities, it established the first U.S. postwar bank branches in Germany and Japan. These branches joined existing Chase branches in London and Paris and were followed by the opening of others around the world. In the 1970s, Chase added nearly 40 new branches, representative offices, affiliates, subsidiaries and joint ventures outside the United States. These included two historic firsts in 1973: Chase opened a representative office in Moscow – the first Russian presence of an American bank since the 1920s – and, in the same year, Chase became the first U.S. correspondent to the Bank of China since the 1949 Chinese Revolution.

Chase's postwar expansion was led by David Rockefeller, who joined the bank in 1946 as assistant manager of the Foreign Department after having served in Army intelligence during World War II. He was elected vice president of Chase in 1949, president in 1961, and chairman and chief executive officer in 1969.

Below left: In 1973, Chase Manhattan Bank Chairman David Rockefeller visited China and met with Chinese Prime Minister Chou En-Lai. Chase became the first U.S. correspondent to the Bank of China since the 1949 Chinese Revolution.

Below right: Chase National Bank was one of the first banks to appreciate the potential market for American banks in international trade, responding with a postwar advertising campaign promoting its capabilities abroad.

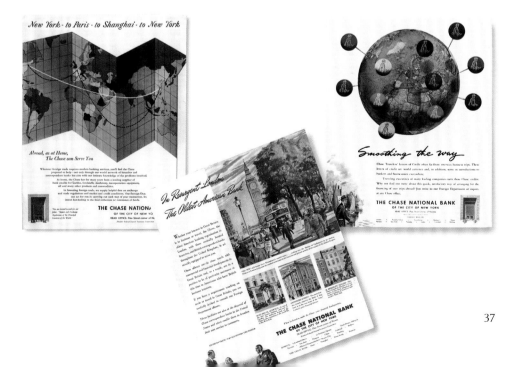

A demand deposit with Morgan Guaranty opens doors around the world

London

Paris

Morgan Guaranty Trust Co. of New York also was noteworthy in its pursuit of international growth. Prior to its merger with Guaranty Trust Company in 1959, J.P. Morgan & Co. had retained a one-third interest in London merchant bank Morgan Grenfell & Co., while Guaranty maintained the London office it had opened in 1897. These operations were a platform for global expansion. By 1965, Morgan Guaranty had five overseas branches, and by 1978, it had 16.

To complement its branches, Morgan bought minority stakes in foreign banks under the terms of the U.S. Edge Act, a law that allowed banks to form subsidiaries for overseas investment. Morgan Guaranty created two Edge Act subsidiaries in 1960. Within two years, the subsidiaries owned interests in banks in 11 countries, including Argentina, the Bahamas, Morocco, Taiwan and Australia. A Morgan spokesperson told *The New York Times*: "Through our Edge Act subsidiaries, we can now provide our customers who want to expand abroad with a calling card that will give them entry into those financial houses where our subsidiaries have acquired ownership interests."

Many American banks brought innovative ideas to the countries in which they opened branches. In 1968, the Brussels office of Morgan Guaranty launched Euroclear, the first electronic settlement service for Eurobond transactions. The new service helped support the growth of Eurobond trading and made global investing easier. Today, Euroclear is owned by its users and is the world's largest clearing system for international securities.

Among JPMorgan Chase & Co.'s predecessors in the Midwest, The First National Bank of Chicago was the most active internationally, establishing offices in 25 countries by 1973.

Above left: Morgan Guaranty Trust Co. of New York advertisements, like this one from 1970, promoted the firm's growing global business in local markets throughout the world.

Above middle and right: In 1960, the newly formed Morgan Guaranty opened a second London branch, on Berkeley Square. J.P. Morgan acquired its Paris office, on the historic Place Vendôme, in 1917. It remains the firm's main office in France today.

U.S. bank consolidation

Below: In 1955, Chase National Bank, the third-largest bank in the United States, merged with the much smaller Bank of The Manhattan Co. The merger combined Chase's strength in international, corporate and correspondent banking with The Bank of The Manhattan Co.'s large New York City branch network.

Background photo: In 1961, Manufacturers Trust Co., which had one of the largest branch networks in New York, merged with The Hanover Bank, a wholesale and correspondent bank with a sizable trust business and a relatively small retail branch system.

In addition to globalization, a second major postwar trend in the United States was industry consolidation through mergers, acquisitions and the formation of multi-bank holding companies.

In New York City, a wave of mergers created a few big banks serving many customers through extensive branch networks. All four of JPMorgan Chase's major New York City heritage firms – J.P. Morgan & Co., The Chase Manhattan Bank, Manufacturers Hanover Trust Co. and Chemical Bank – grew through mergers in the 1950s.

After passage of the 1956 Bank Holding Company Act, all four firms created holding companies and helped shape the industry for decades. The new law allowed holding companies owning just one bank to diversify into some non-banking activities.

First Banc Group of Ohio, formed in 1968, was one of the most innovative and successful multi-bank holding companies in the nation. It was created by City National Bank & Trust Co. of Columbus and Farmers Saving & Trust Co., a smaller Ohio bank. First Banc Group acquired banks throughout Ohio and later extended its acquisitions to Arizona, Colorado, Indiana, Texas, Utah, Wisconsin and other states. The company later changed its name to Bank One Corp.

39

Development of credit cards

Below left: By 1969, the Chase Manhattan Bank Charge Plan – CMCP – was the leading bank credit card in the New York City metropolitan area.

Below middle: City National Bank & Trust Co. of Columbus saw the advantages of a national all-purpose credit card when it began offering a City National BankAmericard in 1966.

Below right: Manufacturers Hanover Trust Co. was deluged with applications from bank customers when it began offering Master Charge credit cards in New York in 1969.

Although the first multi-use credit card was launched by Diners Club in 1950, credit cards did not gain widespread public acceptance in the United States until the late 1960s. Several JPMorgan Chase predecessors played key roles.

In 1958, The Chase Manhattan Bank introduced the Chase Manhattan Bank Charge Plan, becoming the first New York City bank, and one of the first in the nation, to offer customers a single retail charge account that provided credit at a citywide network of stores.

In 1966, shortly before founding First Banc Group of Ohio, City National Bank & Trust Co. of Columbus became one of the first banks outside California to introduce BankAmericard, the precursor of Visa. Five years later, City National was involved in the first major national test of point-of-sale terminals for processing credit card transactions.

Manufacturers Hanover Trust Co. and Chemical Bank entered the national credit card business in 1969 as founding members of the Eastern States Bankcard Association. This group linked up with other regional bank groups to form a nationwide network that began issuing cards under the Master Charge plan (now MasterCard), a direct competitor of BankAmericard.

In 1981, Bank One received national attention for linking its Visa credit cards and data processing technology to several major brokerage firms' money market funds, giving customers access to their money market accounts through their Visa cards. Propelled in part by the popularity of this new service, Bank One became the nation's largest processor of Visa card transactions.

ATMs and debit cards

Banking soon emerged as one of the nation's most innovative industries. Capitalizing on advances in technology, banks launched a host of new products and services that offered customers greater convenience, value and choice.

JPMorgan Chase predecessors were instrumental in introducing automated teller machines (ATM), which revolutionized banking. In 1969, Chemical Bank installed the first prototype cash-dispensing machine in America, a precursor of the ATM, becoming the first bank in the country to allow customers to withdraw cash 24 hours a day. City National Bank & Trust Co. of Columbus also embraced the emerging technology, installing the first production model cash-dispensing machines in 1970.

Several other JPMorgan Chase predecessors were involved in forming early electronic banking networks to enable customers to withdraw funds from ATMs, not only at their own banks but at competitor banks as well. Washington Mutual formed The Exchange,

the first such network in the mid-1970s, with 16 other banks in the Pacific Northwest.

The idea caught on quickly. Marine National Exchange Bank of Milwaukee helped establish TYME (Take Your Money Everywhere) in Wisconsin; National Bank of Detroit was a founder of METROMONEY, the first shared electronic bank terminal program in Michigan; and in 1985, Chemical Bank and Manufacturers Hanover Trust Co. were among the founders of NYCE (New York Cash Exchange), the first automated teller network in the New York metropolitan area. As networks expanded their geographic reach, customers eventually were able to conduct banking transactions from almost any ATM in the world.

Bank debit cards, introduced in the late 1970s, enabled customers to withdraw cash from ATMs, pay for retail purchases with a card in lieu of a check and access additional banking services. The Chase Manhattan Bank introduced the Chase Money Card – the first Visa debit card offered by a bank in New York.

Home banking by computer

Home banking was another major innovation. Several of JPMorgan Chase's predecessors played key roles in its early development. In 1976, Washington Mutual pioneered Pay-by-Phone, which allowed customers to pay their bills by phoning a computer and using the telephone keypad to enter instructions such as the amount to be paid and the code number for the recipient of the payment.

Four years later, Bank One developed and tested another early version of home banking. Called Channel 2000, it allowed bank customers to view their bank and department store balances on a television screen, pay bills and shift money among accounts. The service worked over regular telephone lines; the Internet, which is used today for home banking, was not commercialized until 1987.

JPMorgan Chase's predecessors were innovators of early home banking technologies. Bank One tested Channel 2000 in 1980; Chase Manhattan launched Spectrum in 1985.

In 1983, Chemical Bank introduced Pronto, the first major full-fledged online banking service. Using a home computer, modem and software, customers could pay bills, transfer funds, review account balances, track budgets and balance their checkbooks. After establishing the service in New York, Chemical began licensing it to banks around the country and later introduced a version for small businesses.

In 1985, The Chase Manhattan Bank launched its electronic home banking service, called Spectrum, which not only permitted banking transactions but also allowed customers to buy and sell stocks through a discount broker affiliated with Chase.

Left: A precursor of computer banking, Washington Mutual's Pay-by-Phone service, introduced in 1976, enabled customers to pay an unlimited number of bills each month by using any telephone, and the bank offered extended hours to do so.

Difficult competitive environment

Banks weren't the only financial institutions that launched new products and services. The restrictions imposed on U.S. banks by Glass-Steagall began to erode in the 1970s as competition from non-banking institutions and the growing role of technology drove change throughout the financial services sector. Innovative financial products were launched by brokers, mutual fund companies, savings banks and other providers – products that enabled customers to earn higher returns on their money and enjoy greater flexibility in managing their assets. Many of these products competed with savings accounts, checking accounts and other banking services.

In this environment of innovation and prolific change, regulatory policies such as rate regulation, originally aimed at protecting banks, handicapped their ability to compete. The deregulation of rates paid by banks to savers began slowly. In 1978, the Federal Reserve authorized banks to issue a novel product: the six-month money market certificate with a variable rate ceiling tied to six-month Treasury bills. Nearly all of JPMorgan Chase's predecessor banks offered these certificates.

Later that same year, banks were authorized to introduce "sweep" services, overcoming the long-standing prohibition against paying interest on checking accounts. This helped banks compete with brokerage firm sweep programs and thrift institutions' interest-paying NOW checking accounts, which combined checking and savings in a single account. When, in 1979, commercial banks received regulatory approval to offer NOW checking accounts, The Chase Manhattan Bank was among the first to introduce the innovative service.

Spurred in part by this piecemeal and sometimes complex deregulation, Congress passed the Depository Institutions Deregulation and Monetary Control Act of 1980, which phased out all savings rate ceilings on consumer accounts, completely removing, over the next six years, the rate ceilings imposed by Glass-Steagall.

CHRONICLE

Jan./Feb. 1988

For the Employees of Chemical Bank, Texas Commerce Bancshares and their Affiliates

INVESTMENT BANKERS ONLY!
COMMERCIAL BANKERS KEEP OUT
BY ORDER OF U.S. CONGRESS
(GLASS-STEAGALL ACT, 1933)

More Cracks In Glass-Steagall
Underwriting Puts Banks In New Arena

By SHIRLEY HOBBS SCHEIBLA

WASHINGTON—As President Reagan observed at the Berlin Wall, not even the Wall of Jericho came down all at once. The same applies to the wall between commercial and investment banking established by the Glass-Steagall Act. But some important crumbling has taken place recently.

One generated headlines last week when the Supreme Court let stand an appeals court's ruling that Bankers Trust Co. may sell commercial paper for its clients. These unsecured, short-term borrowings have become a multibillion-dollar enterprise for investment bankers. Now they will face increasing competition from commercial bankers for this part of the securities business. An allied case is now pending at an appeals court involving the Federal Reserve's ruling that subsidiaries of bank holding companies may underwrite as well as sell such securities.

Another recent crumbling was hardly noticed, but perhaps just as important because it involves underwriting of corporate bonds by commercial banks, heretofore deemed forbidden by Glass-Steagall. On June 18, a seemingly routine tombstone ad announced a $150 million, seven-year note issued by the little-known Private Export Funding Corp. But close reading reveals that, for the first time, a commercial bank, J.P. Morgan, heads the list of underwriters. Other co-lead underwriters include Bankers Trust and Citicorp, as well as Dillon Read & Co., Merrill Lynch and Salomon Brothers. Eight other commercial banks displaced a couple of dozen securities firms as the rest of the underwriters.

The corporation, known as PEFCO, determined that this is legal because its obligations are backed by the full faith and credit of the U.S. government, making them just as safe, if not safer, than municipal bonds and federal agency issues, which banks already underwrite.

But what is PEFCO and what qualifies it for such impressive backing? It was incorporated back in 1970, at the suggestion of Dillon Read, as a way of supplementing Export-Import Bank loans to stimulate U.S. exports. The idea was to establish a source of intermediate-term credit. The owners of PEFCO include most of the major U.S. commercial banks in export financing—49, to be exact—seven manufacturers and Dillon Read, which has about 1% equity.

Donald B. Riefler, a member of PEFCO's board and chairman of the Sources and Uses of Funds Committee of Morgan Guaranty Trust, the principal subsidiary of J.P. Morgan, explains that PEFCO was set up with the export of Boeing's 747s in mind. Intermediate-term credit was called for, averaging six or seven years. Then, as now, Eximbank was limited in the amount of direct lending it could do, concentrating more on loan guarantees; PEFCO doesn't labor under stifling federal budgetary restraints, as does Eximbank.

The corporation has a small staff and depends upon commercial bankers to find loan customers. Usually the banks are willing to lend one to three years. On longer maturities, they often go to PEFCO, which, in turn, depends completely upon Eximbank to make each credit decision. Once it obtains Eximbank approval, PEFCO makes the loan. Terms and rates depend upon PEFCO's costs of borrowing in the bond market.

The rates usually are...

MONEY & MARKETS
UNLEASHING BANKS ON WALL STREET

Barred ever since the Great Depression from most securities underwriting, commercial bankers may soon get the chance to go after a big piece of it. The big losers: investment bankers. The big winners: people who want to raise money.

■ *by Robert E. Norton*

BANKERS are readying an assault on one of Wall Street's most cherished domains: securities underwriting. The betting in Washington is that, before the year is out, the Federal Reserve Board will permit banking companies to expand into several underwriting businesses. Among the possibilities are commercial paper, municipal revenue bonds, and securities backed by mortgages and consumer loans, which together represent three-fourths of the $540 billion a year in financing now off limits to these institutions. The Fed will be blasting the biggest hole yet in the 53-year-old Glass-Steagall Act separating U.S. commercial and investment banking.

That is good news for borrowers, for the added competition should drive down the cost of financing. The banks, which have stood by while investment houses made off with more and more of the nation's financing business, can hardly wait to move into the new territory. Bankers Trust is all set to unveil an underwriting subsidiary, and a special securities unit of the J.P. Morgan bank holding company—so far confined to government bond trading and limited municipal bond underwriting—is ready to expand. Dennis ... chairman of Morgan's executive ...

from an unsuccessful court battle to keep commercial banks out of discount brokerage two years ago, the investment banks are trying—vainly, it appears—to dissuade regulators from allowing another ...

The bankers ret... atypical—and ... they fo...

In the vanguard: Dennis Weatherstone of the Morgan bank is eager fo...

MERGER CHIEF: Roberto G. Mendoza

Restoring Morgan To Its Original Role

'We're playing for the financial market of the year 2000, not next week's rankings.'

The New York Times/Neal Boenzi

AMERICAN MANUFACTURERS QUESTION WHY FREE ENTERPRISE DOESN'T APPLY TO AMERICAN BANKS.

Recently, the 13,500 members of the National Association of Manufacturers publicly declared that existing banking law must change.

They called for repeal of the Glass-Steagall Act, the 1933 law which erected an artificial barrier between commercial and investment banking. The law which restrains America's commercial banks from competing in today's radically changed financial environment.

Why on earth would a textile manufacturer in North Carolina or a steel company in Ohio care about banks?

"Competition will stimulate new and innovative services and produce lower costs in the financial markets. Manufacturers have borne additional cost because of artificial constraints."

The N.A.M.'s raison d'être is to promote American business and healthy competition. But clearly, like every other user of financial services, they stand to benefit from banks competing as equal players in the industry.

Manufacturers are hardly alone in questioning the value of Glass-Steagall's restrictions. Increasingly, with supporters drawn from other diverse vocational legislators, regulators, academicians, the media, the Administration, and, naturally, America's banks.

An astonishing 77% of business executives in nonfinancial firms support repeal, according to a recent Senate banking committee survey.

What could account for such an overwhelming consensus?

"The consumer loses, denied the benefits of full competition."

When the Congress of 1933 erected a wall between underwriting and lending, it could never have foreseen how profoundly financial matters would change. How the law would lock banks out of supplying what others in financial services can routinely provide.

Or how such restraint would leave nearly 65% of this country's corporate debt and equity underwriting in the hands of just five investment banks.

Or how hamstringing commercial banks would make the U.S. woefully uncompetitive in a world marketplace.

"It seems inevitable that institutional deregulation will eventually arrive in the United States...However, the longer Glass-Steagall restrictions are kept in place, the more my own country stands to benefit."

It is rather telling that some of the most vocal arguments for repeal come from the leaders of the federal agencies charged with protecting bank safety and soundness. The Federal Reserve Board Chairman. The U.S. Comptroller of the Currency. The FDIC.

So much for the unfounded fears that allowing bank holding companies to operate securities subsidiaries would mean increased risk for bank depositors.

Quite surprising, however, is backing from another source.

"...if one discounts those attempting to protect themselves from ever-increasing competition, there is an overwhelming consensus for restructuring the financial services industry."

Though there is such dissent in the ranks, the only major camp opposing deregulation is the Securities industry associations—the lobby charged with protecting the investment banks' turf. Their opposition is scarcely unexpected.

The real barrier remains inertia. Understanding reform of the financial services industry is a difficult task. But today, it is an essential one.

"We now have an historic opportunity to put the financial system on a sounder footing...to make it more responsive to consumer needs, more efficient, more competitive in the world economy, and equally important, more stable."

It's time to overhaul our nation's outmoded banking laws. Chase believes the constraints of American banks have been denied the benefits of free enterprise for far too long.

Let banks compete.

INERTIA IS FAR MORE DANGEROUS THAN CHANGE

□ CHASE

Repeal of Glass-Steagall

Another fundamental element of Glass-Steagall – the wall between commercial and investment banking – crumbled in response to market change, and JPMorgan Chase heritage institutions were in the center of the action. In 1987, The Chase Manhattan Corp. became the first commercial banking institution to receive Federal Reserve approval to underwrite commercial paper – unsecured short-term corporate debt. Another New York bank previously had been permitted to sell commercial paper as an agent, but Chase was the first to underwrite and deal in these securities for its own account.

The Federal Reserve quickly expanded the scope of the Chase ruling by allowing three major bank holding companies, including J.P. Morgan & Co., to underwrite not only commercial paper but also mortgage-backed securities, municipal revenue bonds and securities backed by consumer receivables.

The Federal Reserve further broadened its rulings in 1989 when it granted J.P. Morgan the authority to underwrite and deal in corporate debt securities in the United States. Morgan was the first commercial bank given this right since Glass-Steagall had been

signed into law in 1933. In 1990, the Federal Reserve approved Morgan's application to underwrite stocks. In the wake of this landmark ruling, Morgan quickly built a leading investment banking operation and, by 1997, was the fourth-largest securities underwriter in the world.

Faced with the reality that the Glass-Steagall barriers were being dismantled by regulators, Congress in 1999 passed the Gramm-Leach-Bliley Act, which removed most of the remaining barriers and allowed financial companies to participate fully across segments. Among other provisions, the new law allowed banks to acquire full-service brokerage and investment banking firms.

Beginning in the 1980s, J.P. Morgan developed its investment banking capability through internal growth. Chase, by contrast, expanded its capability through mergers, starting with the 1999 acquisition of San Francisco investment bank Hambrecht & Quist, a specialist in the technology industry.

Continuing its expansion, in 2000 Chase bought The Beacon Group, a merger and acquisition advisory and private investment firm, and London-based Robert Fleming Holdings, Ltd., an asset management and investment banking concern. Its origins dated back to 1873, when Scotsman Robert Fleming established the first investment trust in Dundee, Scotland, which specialized in investing in American railway bonds. By 2000, when the firm was acquired by Chase, Robert Fleming Holdings managed $100 billion of assets and operated in more than 40 countries.

JP Morgan takes first IPO lead in the US

By Simon London

J. P. Morgan is lead managing its first initial public offering (IPO) of shares since it was granted permission to underwrite equities by the US Federal Reserve Board in September last year.

The bank is leading the international tranche of a 96m share offering for Ayala Land, a Philippine real estate com-

pany. Formed in 1988, Ayala Land is the real estate subsidiary of Ayala Corporation, the Philippines oldest trading company.

Of the shares for sale, 31m are being sold by the parent company and 65m are new. The international tranche amounts to 38m shares, priced at 26 pesos each, equivalent to about $1 per share.

The domestic issue is being lead managed by Bank of the Philippine Islands, in which J. P. Morgan has a 20 per cent stake. The shares will be listed on the Makati and Manila stock exchanges.

J. P. Morgan reported strong Far Eastern demand for the stock, centred on Hong Kong and Singapore. Allocation of shares will close on May 17.

J. P. Morgan was the first of the US money-centre banks to be granted permission to underwrite and deal in equity securities.

In January, the firm lead-managed its first equity offering of any kind – a $58.5m rights issue for Electra Aviation, a privately-owned UK aircraft leasing company.

In addition to straight share offerings, the bank has also been active in equity-related bonds. Last month, it lead managed a $150m subordinated convertible bond offering for Dow Chemical in the US market.

Deregulation and industry consolidation in the United States

The emergence of nationwide branch banking was another change taking place in financial services.

As of 1975, banking in the United States was still primarily a local business. Only 14 states allowed statewide branching, and none permitted out-of-state banks to open branches within their borders. However, pressure for greater branching freedom was mounting, reflecting growing awareness of the consumer convenience of branches, the need for banks to diversify their risks beyond their local markets, and an emerging legislative consensus that deregulation promotes freer markets and greater competition.

Branching deregulation occurred in the 1980s at the state rather than the federal level. In the period from 1975 through 1990, more than 25 additional states – including New York, Ohio, Texas and others in which JPMorgan Chase predecessors operated – authorized statewide branching. In 1984, The Chase Manhattan

Bank ventured to upstate New York by acquiring Lincoln First Banks Inc. in Rochester. Following the transaction, Chase had 330 branches across the state, the largest branch network in New York.

As Illinois anti-branching laws were eased, First Chicago Corp. – the holding company for The First National Bank of Chicago – made a series of acquisitions to expand its business. In 1984, First Chicago acquired Chicago-based American National Corp. and, over the next decade, acquired more than 10 banks and bank holding companies in Illinois.

The 1980s also saw the formation of regional banking zones, representing a major step toward national banking. Banc One Corp. (later Bank One) especially was active in acquiring banks not only in its home state of Ohio but in other states as well. Its first out-of-state acquisition was the purchase of Purdue National Corp. of Lafayette, Indiana, in 1984. By 1994, Banc One Corp. owned 81 banks with more than 1,300 branches in 13 states, including banks in Wisconsin

Above left: This graphic from a 1986 First Chicago Corp. internal newsletter playfully illustrates seven Midwest states that had adopted reciprocal banking legislation. Changes in interstate banking laws permitted cross-border bank acquisitions, which predecessors First Chicago, NBD Bancorp and Bank One aggressively pursued.

Above right: Chemical New York Corporation became a major competitor in Texas after its acquisition of Texas Commerce Bancshares, Inc. in 1987. Texas Commerce had been the premier corporate lender in the Southwest, was a leader in middle market banking and had the biggest affiliate system in the state.

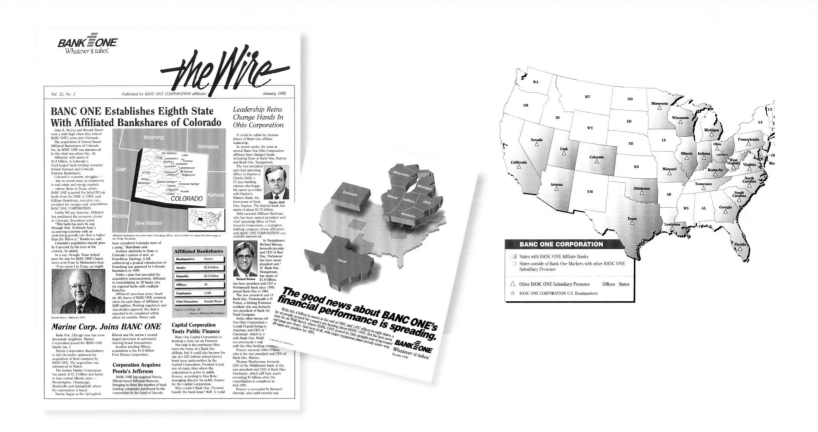

Above: From its first out-of-state acquisition in 1984, Ohio-based Banc One expanded rapidly through affiliations with banks beyond its home state, as illustrated in an employee newsletter, an advertisement and a graphic illustration from the bank's annual report.

(The Marine Corp.), Illinois (Marine Corp.), Colorado (Affiliated Bankshares of Colorado), Kentucky (Liberty National Bancorp), Oklahoma (Central Banking Group), West Virginia (Key Centurion Bancshares), Arizona (Valley National Bank) and Utah (Capital Bancorp). More acquisitions followed.

Banking zones expanded rapidly in geographic size as more states passed reciprocal banking laws. In 1987, Chemical New York Corp. acquired Texas Commerce Bancshares, Inc., the largest interstate banking merger in U.S. history at that time, and First Chicago Corp. acquired Beneficial National Bank USA of Wilmington, Delaware, becoming the third-largest issuer of bank credit cards in the United States.

The growth of banking zones culminated in 1994 with the passage of the federal Riegle-Neal Interstate Banking and Branching Efficiency Act, which made national banking the law of the land. Riegle-Neal allowed bank holding companies to buy banks throughout the United States beginning in the fall of

1995 and permitted nationwide branching – that is, branch offices owned and operated by a single bank – as of June 1997. Many multi-state, multi-bank holding companies soon began to streamline operations by merging their banks. In 1999, Bank One Corp. integrated its banks in Ohio, Michigan, Indiana and Illinois into a single bank with the Bank One name.

The 1990s was a period of intense consolidation for the banking industry; the number of commercial banks in the United States declined to 5,083 as of the end of 2016 from 12,343 at the end of 1990.* However, the number of branches and automated teller machines continued to increase, providing consumers with more banking outlets than ever.

* Source: Federal Financial Institutions Examination Council

Key mergers and acquisitions

Many JPMorgan Chase & Co. predecessors took part in the merger movement that began in the early 1990s. Several significant transactions helped shape the JPMorgan Chase of today:

- In 1991, Chemical Banking Corp. merged with Manufacturers Hanover Corp., keeping the name Chemical Banking Corp., then the second-largest banking institution in the United States.

- In 1995, First Chicago Corp. merged with NBD Bancorp Inc., forming First Chicago NBD Corp., the largest banking company based in the Midwest.

- In 1996, Chemical Banking Corp. merged with The Chase Manhattan Corp., keeping the name The Chase Manhattan Corp. and creating what then was the largest bank holding company in the United States.

- In 1998, Banc One Corp. merged with First Chicago NBD Corp., taking the name Bank One Corp. Merging subsequently with Louisiana's First Commerce Corp., Bank One became the largest financial services firm in the Midwest, the fourth-largest bank in the United States and the world's largest Visa credit card issuer.

1991

John F. McGillicuddy (left)
Manufacturers Hanover Corp.

Walter V. Shipley (right)
Chemical Banking Corp.

1995

Richard L. Thomas (left)
First Chicago Corp.

Vern G. Istock (right)
NBD Bancorp, Inc.

1996

Thomas G. Labrecque (left)
The Chase Manhattan Corp.

Walter V. Shipley (right)
Chemical Banking Corp.

1998

Verne G. Istock (left)
First Chicago NBD Corp.

John B. McCoy (right)
Banc One Corp.

2000

Douglas A. Warner III (left)
J.P. Morgan & Co. Incorporated

William B. Harrison, Jr. (right)
The Chase Manhattan Corp.

2004

Jamie Dimon (left)
Bank One Corp.

William B. Harrison, Jr. (right)
JPMorgan Chase & Co.

- In 2000, The Chase Manhattan Corp. merged with J.P. Morgan & Co. Incorporated, in effect combining four of the largest and oldest money center banking institutions in New York City (Morgan, Chase, Chemical and Manufacturers Hanover) into one firm called JPMorgan Chase & Co.

- In 2004, Bank One Corp. merged with JPMorgan Chase & Co., keeping the name JPMorgan Chase & Co. *The New York Times* reported the merger "would realign the competitive landscape for banks" by uniting the investment and commercial banking skills of JPMorgan Chase with the consumer banking strengths of Bank One. The merger enlarged JPMorgan Chase's retail presence to 17 states across the United States.

- In 2008, JPMorgan Chase & Co. acquired The Bear Stearns Companies Inc., strengthening the company's capabilities across a broad range of businesses, including prime brokerage, cash clearing and energy trading globally.

- In 2008, JPMorgan Chase also acquired certain deposits and assets of Seattle-based savings and loan Washington Mutual. The acquisition included the bank's 2,200 U.S. branches, expanding JPMorgan Chase's retail presence to 23 states from coast to coast.

- In 2010, J.P. Morgan acquired full ownership of its U.K. joint venture, J.P. Morgan Cazenove, one of Britain's premier investment banks.

Financial crisis of 2008

JPMorgan Chase remained profitable throughout the 2008 financial crisis, in large part owing to a fortress balance sheet – a hallmark of JPMorgan Chase Chairman and CEO Jamie Dimon's management philosophy.

In his 2009 annual letter to JPMorgan Chase shareholders, Dimon wrote, "When the global financial crisis unfolded in 2008, the people of JPMorgan Chase understood the vital role our firm needed to play and felt a deep responsibility to our many stakeholders. It is this sense of responsibility that enables us to move beyond the distractions of the moment and stay focused on what really matters: taking care of our clients, helping the communities in which we operate and protecting our company."

Major predecessors of JPMorgan Chase & Co. since 1799

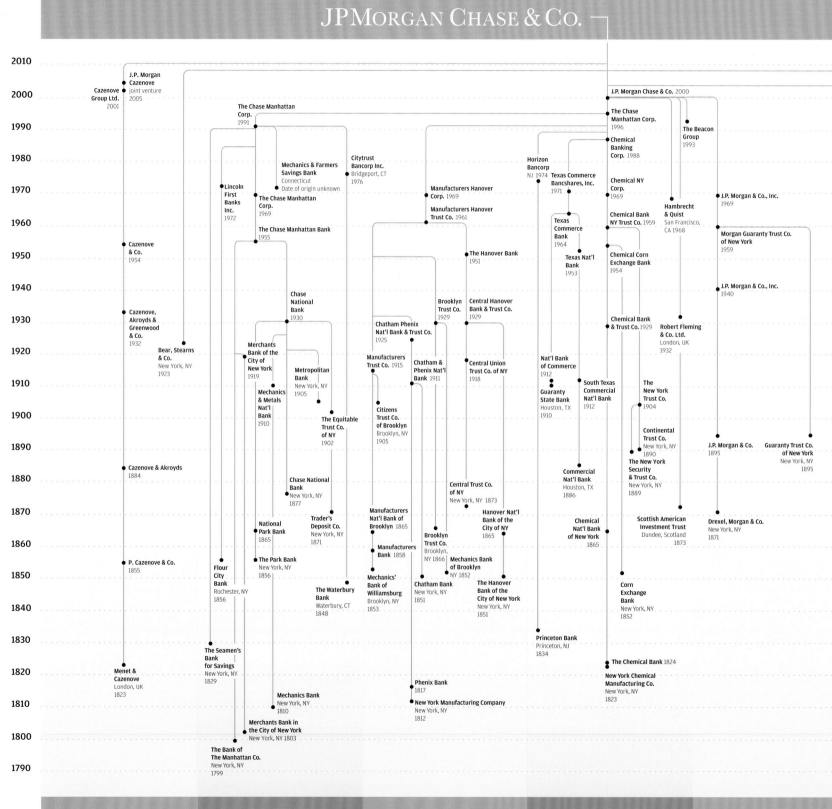

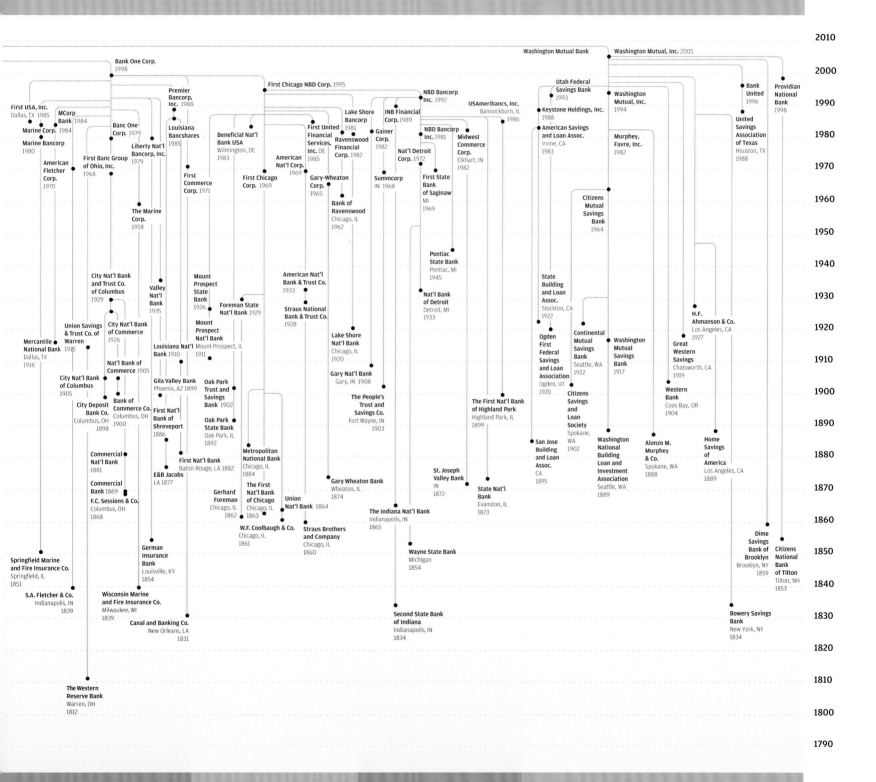

2010

2000

Washington Mutual Bank   Washington Mutual, Inc. 2005

Bank One Corp.
1998

First Chicago NBD Corp. 1995

NBD Bancorp
Inc. 1992

Utah Federal
Savings Bank
1993

Washington
Mutual, Inc.

Bank
United
1996

Providian
National
Bank
1998

2000

1990

Premier
Bancorp,
Inc. 1988

USAmeribancs, Inc.
Bannockburn, IL
1986

Keystone Holdings, Inc.
1988

Washington
Mutual, Inc.
1994

First USA, Inc.
Dallas, TX 1985

MCorp
Bank 1984

Lake Shore
Bancorp
1981

INB Financial
Corp. 1989

American Savings
and Loan Assoc.
Irvine, CA
1983

United
Savings
Association
of Texas
Houston, TX
1988

1990

Marine Corp. 1984

Banc One
Corp. 1979

Louisiana
Bancshares
1985

Beneficial Nat'l
Bank USA
Wilmington, DE
1983

First United
Financial
Services,
Inc. DE
1985

Ravenswood
Financial
Corp. 1982

Gainer
Corp.
1982

NBD Bancorp
Inc. 1981

Midwest
Commerce
Corp.
Elkhart, IN
1982

Murphey,
Favre, Inc.
1982

1980

Marine Bancorp
1980

Liberty Nat'l
Bancorp, Inc.

American
Nat'l Corp.
1969

Nat'l Detroit
Corp. 1972

1980

American
Fletcher
Corp.
1970

First Banc Group
of Ohio, Inc.
1968

First
Commerce
Corp. 1971

First Chicago
Corp. 1969

Gary-Wheaton
Corp.
1965

Summcorp
IN 1968

First State
Bank
of Saginaw
MI
1969

1970

The Marine
Corp.
1958

Bank of
Ravenswood
Chicago, IL
1962

Citizens
Mutual
Savings
Bank
1964

1960

1950

Pontiac
State Bank
Pontiac, MI
1945

1940

City Nat'l Bank
and Trust Co.
of Columbus
1929

Valley
Nat'l
Bank
1935

Mount
Prospect
State
Bank
1926

American Nat'l
Bank & Trust Co.
1933

Nat'l Bank
of Detroit
Detroit, MI
1933

State
Building
and Loan
Assoc.
Stockton, CA
1922

H.F.
Ahmanson & Co.
Los Angeles, CA
1927

1930

Union Savings
& Trust Co. of
Warren

City Nat'l Bank
of Commerce
1926

Foreman State
Nat'l Bank 1929

Straus National
Bank & Trust Co.
1928

Ogden
First
Federal
Savings
and Loan
Association
Ogden, UT
1920

Continental
Mutual
Savings
Bank
Seattle, WA
1920

Washington
Mutual
Savings
Bank
1922

Great
Western
Savings
Chatsworth, CA
1919

1920

Mercantile
National Bank
Dallas, TX
1916

Mount
Prospect
Nat'l Bank
Mount Prospect, IL
1911

Lake Shore
Nat'l Bank
Chicago, IL
1920

1910

Louisiana Nat'l
Bank 1910

City Nat'l Bank
of Columbus
1905

Nat'l Bank of
Commerce 1905

Gila Valley Bank
Phoenix, AZ 1899

Oak Park
Trust and
Savings
Bank 1902

Gary Nat'l Bank
Gary, IN 1908

Citizens
Savings
and
Loan
Society
Spokane,
WA
1902

Western
Bank
Coos Bay, OR
1904

1900

City Deposit
Bank Co.
Columbus, OH
1898

Bank of
Commerce Co.
Columbus, OH
1900

First Nat'l
Bank of
Shreveport
1886

Oak Park
State Bank
Oak Park, IL
1892

The People's
Trust and
Savings Co.
Fort Wayne, IN
1903

The First Nat'l Bank
of Highland Park
Highland Park, IL
1899

1890

Commercial
Nat'l Bank
1881

First Nat'l Bank
Baton Rouge, LA 1882

Metropolitan
National Bank
Chicago, IL
1884

San Jose
Building
and Loan
Assoc.
CA
1895

Washington
National
Building
Loan and
Investment
Association
Seattle, WA
1889

Alonzo M.
Murphey
& Co.
Spokane, WA
1888

Home
Savings
of
America
Los Angeles, CA
1889

1880

Commercial
Bank 1869

E&B Jacobs
LA 1877

The First
Nat'l Bank
of Chicago
Chicago, IL
1863

Gary Wheaton Bank
Wheaton, IL
1874

1870

F.C. Sessions & Co.
Columbus, OH
1868

Gerhard
Foreman
Chicago, IL
1862

Union
Nat'l Bank 1864

St. Joseph
Valley Bank
IN
1872

State Nat'l
Bank
Evanston, IL
1873

Dime
Savings
Bank of
Brooklyn
Brooklyn, NY
1859

Citizens
National
Bank
of Tilton
Tilton, NH
1853

1860

W.F. Coolbaugh & Co.
Chicago, IL
1861

Straus Brothers
and Company
Chicago, IL
1860

The Indiana Nat'l Bank
Indianapolis, IN
1865

1850

German
Insurance
Bank
Louisville, KY
1854

Wayne State Bank
Michigan
1854

Springfield Marine
and Fire Insurance Co.
Springfield, IL
1851

1840

S.A. Fletcher & Co.
Indianapolis, IN
1839

Wisconsin Marine
and Fire Insurance Co.
Milwaukee, WI
1839

Second State Bank
of Indiana
Indianapolis, IN
1834

Bowery Savings
Bank
New York, NY
1834

1830

Canal and Banking Co.
New Orleans, LA
1831

1820

1810

The Western
Reserve Bank
Warren, OH
1812

1800

1790

Two iconic brands

Since the formation of JPMorgan Chase & Co. in 2000, the firm has operated its wholesale and retail banking businesses under two brands – J.P. Morgan and Chase. Under this dual-brand strategy, the company's Corporate & Investment Bank and Asset & Wealth Management businesses fall under the J.P. Morgan brand and Consumer & Community Banking – which includes U.S. Retail Banking, Card Services & Auto and Mortgage Banking – and Commercial Banking under the Chase brand. Both have a strong heritage and powerful brand equity in the financial services world. In addition, each of the two brand marks used by the firm is associated with a long tradition of innovation, high performance standards, integrity, client service and commitment to relationships.

J.P. Morgan has remained one of the most respected and trusted names in financial services. In 2008, J.P. Morgan introduced a new logo to reflect its rich history, reinforcing the firm's connection to its namesake, J. Pierpont Morgan. He embodied traits – character, intelligence and strength – that the firm still embraces today. In recent years, several studies have ranked the J.P. Morgan brand among the most valuable brands in the world.*

* Source: Interbrand, Best Global Brands 2016; *Forbes*, the World's Most Valuable Brands 2017

J.P.Morgan

The Chase octagon logo was introduced by The Chase Manhattan Bank in 1960 and continues to be the centerpiece of Chase's brand identity. One of the earliest abstract corporate logos, the Chase octagon influenced the widespread adoption of abstract corporate identities. While the color and typeface have evolved over the years, the octagon has been in use continuously since its introduction and remains a powerful and enduring symbol of the Chase brand.

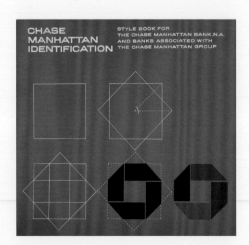

Left: The Chase Manhattan Bank's corporate identity stylebook from 1960 guided employees on the usage of the bank's new octagon logo.

Consumer & Community Banking: A commitment to innovation

Chase has built upon its history of investing in user-friendly technologies by launching innovative new products and services that allow customers to do their banking how, when and where they want. More than a half century ago, ATMs first empowered customers to conduct transactions and have 24-hour access to their money without visiting their local bank branch. Today, four out of five Chase customer transactions are completed using self-service devices. Tens of millions of Chase customers routinely pay bills, deposit checks, transfer assets among accounts, send and receive money to and from family and friends, complete purchases and conduct other banking transactions using only their phones or other digital devices. And these digitally engaged Chase customers have higher satisfaction and retention rates, spend more and have far lower transaction costs.

Chase invests billions of dollars each year in technology, including several billion dedicated to new initiatives. And, as it continues to focus on what's next for meeting customer needs, Chase has collaborated with innovative fintech companies that have developed ways to simplify the customer experience. Companies like OnDeck, Roostify, TrueCar and Zelle have helped Chase offer faster person-to-person payments to more people; quicker loan decisions for small business customers; online and mobile management of mortgage loans; and the ability to shop for and finance a specific car online and pick it up at a local dealership.

All of this digital activity has not rendered bank branches obsolete – not by a long shot. In fact, Chase continues to build new branches in targeted communities where it sees opportunities to better serve existing customers and attract new ones. About two-thirds of Chase customers visit a branch, on average, more than once a month. Hundreds of millions of transactions each year still are completed the way customers have done it since the dawn of banking – with the help of a teller in a branch. However, the branch experience continues to evolve from historic transaction centers to advice centers. Chase branches today feature more private spaces and conference rooms for customers to meet with a banker and privately discuss their financial needs. Branches also serve as advice centers for millions of small business owners seeking to expand and grow.

Wholesale businesses: Expanding our global scope

J.P. Morgan has continued to expand our presence throughout the world, building upon the international foundation established by our predecessors in the late 19th century.

While others have retrenched in recent years, J.P. Morgan has positioned itself to serve corporate and multinational clients as their ongoing needs to participate in global commerce expand. We have opened new branches in key locations, such as China, Denmark, Finland, Norway, Qatar and Sweden; added services across our platforms; and extended our capabilities in Australia, Europe, India, and the Middle East and Africa. In addition, the firm is expanding its global treasury and securities services, which include transaction, investment and information services such as the third-party custodianship of assets.

Latin America highlights

J.P. Morgan has been serving clients throughout Latin America since 1867. In keeping with the region's growth and recognizing the importance of being close to our clients, the firm has formed a network of offices in Argentina, Brazil, Chile, Colombia, Mexico, Panama, Peru and Venezuela. Argentina also is the home of one of our technology hubs, drawing on the talents and skills in the area to keep J.P. Morgan in the forefront of financial technology.

The firm continues to build on the region's momentum and has forged a significant presence to serve an expanding array of clients, many of whom seek to grow their businesses internationally. In a globalized economy, Latin American corporates are conducting business with partners in Europe, Asia and other countries in the hemisphere that require the services of a bank that can serve their needs across regions.

Europe, Middle East and Africa highlights

Since the 1800s, when the earliest predecessor firms of JPMorgan Chase began their operations in London and Paris, J.P. Morgan has established a sophisticated local market presence throughout Europe, the Middle East and Africa.

Our clients benefit from our global reach, scale and full spectrum of financial products in the region. Those attributes ensure clients that they have the right mix of products and services to carry out their business strategies while relying on our knowledge of local business practices and regulations. The principle of doing business with global reach but local touch has been ingrained in our firm for more than a century.

Asia Pacific highlights

J.P. Morgan holds leading market positions throughout the Asia Pacific region. The firm serves local and multinational corporations, financial institutions and government agencies through a wide range of services across investment banking, risk management, commodities, cash management, trade finance, loans, foreign exchange and derivatives, asset management, futures brokerage and private equity.

The firm is bolstering its on-the-ground presence in China and providing a strong foundation for the business's long-term success in the country:

- J.P. Morgan has branches in major cities throughout China.

- In 2004, the China International Fund Management Co. Ltd. joint venture was formed.

- In 2010, J.P. Morgan received approval from China's securities regulator to establish a joint venture, J.P. Morgan First Capital Securities Company Limited.

- In 2016, J.P. Morgan Asset Management (Shanghai) Ltd. became the first Asset Management Wholly Foreign-Owned Enterprise in Shanghai's free-trade zone.

- In 2017, J.P. Morgan received a corporate bond under-writing license to serve China's interbank market.

In India, J.P. Morgan's businesses include investment banking, commercial banking, and treasury and securities services.

The firm also maintains a substantial presence in Japan, Singapore, Australia and other locations and has large service centers in India and the Philippines that support the firm's businesses worldwide.

JPMorgan Chase & Co. today

Today, JPMorgan Chase & Co. is a leading global financial services firm with operations in more than 60 countries. Its corporate headquarters is located in New York City. Under the J.P. Morgan and Chase brands, the company serves millions of consumers, small businesses, and many of the world's most prominent corporate, institutional and government clients.

Our J.P. Morgan businesses

J.P. Morgan's Corporate & Investment Bank offers a full range of products and services to corporations, financial institutions, governments and institutional investors around the world. J.P. Morgan consistently is ranked among the market leaders across the spectrum of banking, markets and investor services.

With the creation of the Corporate & Investment Bank in 2012, J.P. Morgan aligned its businesses to better serve clients. The Corporate & Investment Bank raises debt and equity and provides credit for clients in more than 100 countries, is the largest clearer of U.S. dollars, provides award-winning research across asset classes and is ranked #1 globally for its Investment Banking fees.* Our Treasury Services business supports approximately 80% of the global Fortune 500 companies, and our Custody & Fund Services business has more than $20 trillion in assets under custody.

Asset & Wealth Management is a global leader in investment and wealth management. Its clients include institutions, retail investors and high-net-worth individuals in every major market around the world. Through the J.P. Morgan Private Bank, J.P. Morgan Securities, J.P. Morgan Asset Management and High-bridge franchises, Asset & Wealth Management offers global investment management in equities, fixed income, real estate, hedge funds, private equity and liquidity, as well as provides trust and estate, banking and brokerage services to high-net-worth clients.

Our Chase businesses

Chase offers a broad range of financial services that help meet the needs of consumers, businesses and midsized corporations across the United States.

Chase Consumer & Community Banking serves about half of all U.S. households and 4 million small businesses. It operates more than 5,000 branches across 23 U.S. states.

Chase Wealth Management includes Chase Private Client and Chase Investments, overseeing more than $250 billion in investment assets.

Home Lending, which includes Retail Lending, Servicing and Real Estate Portfolios, helps people buy, refinance and afford homes. Chase services more than $800 billion in mortgage loans, making it one of the largest mortgage servicers in the United States.

Card Services is the #1 U.S. credit card issuer and the #1 U.S. co-brand credit card issuer and is #1 in U.S. credit and debit payments volume. The firm offers a wide array of general purpose cards to satisfy the needs of individual consumers, small businesses and partner organizations. The division also offers auto loans to individuals and through dealerships.

Chase Merchant Services payment processing volume exceeds $1 trillion per year.

Commercial Banking provides organizations with annual revenue generally ranging from $20 million to more than $2 billion – as well as real estate investors and owners – with a full breadth of domestic and international financial solutions designed to help companies and not-for-profit organizations achieve their business goals.

* Source: Dealogic

**About the JPMorgan Chase
Historical Collection**

Begun in 1975 by Chase Manhattan
Bank Chairman David Rockefeller, the
JPMorgan Chase Historical Collection
is one of the oldest corporate history
programs in the United States. Recognized
as an important corporate asset and an
invaluable resource for financial history,
the Historical Collection has continually
advanced the firm's rich legacy by
collecting and preserving historical
materials of JPMorgan Chase & Co.
and its more than 1,200 predecessor
institutions worldwide.

With more than 12,000 feet of records,
this extensive collection of documents
and artifacts traces the remarkable
origins, developments and achievements
of the firm from 1799 to the present
and highlights key events and business
decisions, offering valuable insight into
the firm's mission and vision.

**Director
JPMorgan Chase
Historical Collection**
Jean Elliott

Writers
Dick Blodgett
Nancy Palley

Designer
Gerben Hooykaas

Acknowledgments
Kate Cadette, Neila Radin
and John Stewart
for their editorial input

The People

of the State of New York by the Grace of Go[d]

Know Ye, That WE having Inspected

of the Legislature of our said State in the words and figures following, to wit; "An
" Ludlow and John B Church together with sundry other Citizens of this State have As[s]
" bitants thereof and others as may be inclined to take the same; and have with a view to fur[ther]
" scription, and actually subscribed considerable sums of money thereto, upon condition
" by giving them and such others as shall hereafter subscribe and Join their association
" To the end therefore, that the said Daniel Ludlow and John B Church and their present a[nd]
" which promises under the blessing of God to be conducive to the future health and safety [of]
" Represented in Senate and Assembly, That Daniel Ludlow, John B Church, John Wa[tts]
" they are hereby Created a Body Corporate and politic by the name of the "President and
" to be forever hereafter, a Body politic and Corporate in fact and in name, and by that na[me]
" in Law Capable of suing and being sued pleading and being impleaded, answering
" in all manner of Actions, suits, complaints, matters and Causes whatsoever; and th[e]
" at their pleasure; And also that they and their Successors by the same name and s[t]
" al for the use of the said Corporation. Provided that the Real Estate so to be h[eld]
" And be it further enacted, That the Capital Stock of the said Corporation shall
" Dollars; and that Subscriptions to the said Capital Stock shall be opened and kept op[en]
" subscribed, together with those already subscribed shall amount to thirty nine Thousar[d]
" for the Benefit of such Persons as may choose to subscribe for not more than two sha[res]
" of New York, to subscribe to the said Stock any Number of Shares not exceeding
" the said Company shall be conducted and managed by thirteen Directors, Stock[holders]
" of New York for the time being shall always, ex officio, be one, which Directors shall ho[ld]
" Directors shall be elected on the first Tuesday in December in every year at such time
" being shall appoint and public notice shall be given by the said Directors not less than
" least two of the public newspapers printed in the said City of New York, and the said
" purpose in their proper persons or by proxy, and all Elections for directors shall be by
" be the Directors. And if it shall happen at any Election that two or more persons ha[ve]
" by plurality of Votes appear to be chosen as Directors, then the said Stockholders h[ave]
" plurality of Votes determine which of the persons so having an equal Number of Votes